English Wills

English Wills

Probate Records in England and Wales
With a Brief Note on
Scottish and Irish Wills

by

PETER WALNE, M.A.
County Archivist of Hertford

A SPECIAL REPORT

OF THE

VIRGINIA COLONIAL RECORDS PROJECT

THE VIRGINIA STATE LIBRARY
RICHMOND, VIRGINIA

First edition 1964.
Reprinted by the Virginia State Library 1981.

Library of Congress Cataloging in Publication Data

Walne, Peter.
English wills.

"A special report of the Virginia colonial records project."
Reprint. Originally published: Richmond, Va.: Virginia State Library, 1964. (Virginia State Library publications; no. 23)
Includes bibliographical references.
1. Wills—Great Britain. 2. Probate records—Great Britain. 3. Ecclesiastical courts—Great Britain. I. Title. II. Series: Virginia State Library publications; no. 23.
[KD1509.W35 1981] 346.4205'4 81-10478
ISBN 0-88490-097-5 AACR2

Standard Book Number: 0-88490-097-5
Virginia State Library, Richmond, Virginia.

FOR

LEWIS F. POWELL, JR.

IN APPRECIATION OF HIS MANY SERVICES

AS MEMBER OF THE

LIBRARY BOARD OF VIRGINIA

1954 - 1964

PREFATORY NOTE

TO THE SECOND EDITION

In 1960 the Virginia State Library published four special reports of the Virginia Colonial Records Project in one volume under the title *The British Public Record Office.* Four years later the Library published the first edition of Peter Walne's guide to the possible locations of American wills that might have been recorded in England as late as 1858. The Virginia Committee on Colonial Records was primarily responsible for this informative report, which was prepared under the direction of George H. Reese. The Appendix to this second edition has been revised to reflect changes in locations and addresses of pre-1858 English and Welsh probate records.

JON KUKLA

INTRODUCTION

This Special Report, prepared by Mr. Peter Walne, County Archivist of Hertford, was commissioned by the Virginia Colonial Records Project. The purpose was to describe as briefly as possible English probate procedures, and to dispel the prevalent misconceptions concerning American wills of the colonial period probated in England. As the author indicates, only the wills of persons dying in the colonies or at sea who left property in England or Wales would fall under English probate jurisdiction. In such cases the will might be found in the Prerogative Court of Canterbury, or, in a few instances, in the Prerogative Court of York.

Those accustomed to the civil probate of wills have some difficulty in understanding the probate of wills by ecclesiastical courts as practiced in England before 1858. This is explained in the Special Report in as much detail as space permits. Mr. Walne starts by discussing the structure of the Church of England from bottom to top, and indicates the probate jurisdiction for each unit. Particular attention is given to the Prerogative Court of Canterbury. Although the incidence of American colonial wills is small, the Special Report should be useful for those interested in the wills of English ancestors, how these wills were probated and the whereabouts of these wills.

The Virginia Colonial Records Project did not obtain microfilm or other copies of wills of Virginia interest from the Principal Probate Registry at Somerset House or any other repository. Enquiries about such wills should be directed to the repository where the wills are probably to be found.

William J. Van Schreeven
Virginia State Archivist and
Chairman, Virginia Committee on
Colonial Records

CONTENTS

Introductory

¤

THE story of wills and probate of wills in England and Wales before 1858 is one of considerable complexity and difficulty. The aim of this Special Report is to give as simple an explanation of the subject as its complexity will permit, by discussing in turn the courts in which wills might be proved, the stages in the proving of a will and the subsidiary documents produced in the course of this transaction, and the whereabouts of probate documents today, with some general remarks which may be of value to those who resort to probate records for historical purposes.

It should be understood at the start that this report is concerned almost exclusively with the practices current in England and Wales before 1858, and that Scotland and Ireland were independent in the matter of wills. A brief note on Scottish and Irish wills and probates, and some notes on English and Welsh probate records and courts after 1858, are added to the report for completeness' sake.

It is hoped that, among other things, this report will serve to do away with the widespread misconception that all English and Welsh wills, irrespective of date, are in the Principal Probate Registry at Somerset House and, specifically, that all Virginian wills for the colonial period can automatically and with no difficulty be located in Somerset House.

This report does not pretend to be an exhaustive account of the matters with which it deals, for such an account would require at least one fair-sized volume; but it attempts to be accurate, adequate and straightforward enough, without going into excessive technical and legal detail, to make the involved history of wills and their probates in England and Wales before 1858 comprehensible to the person who wishes to know where a will might be found and why.

The Probate of Wills Before 1858

☼

THE Court of Probate Act, 1857 (20 and 21 Victoria, cap. 77) brought to an end the complex system of proving wills which had grown up in England and Wales since the later Middle Ages, substituting for it a centralized rational system. Before 1858 the proving of a will, the ratification by a competent authority which was essential to make the terms of the will operative and effective in law, might have been undertaken by any one of a considerable number of courts competent in law to grant a probate of a will, or to authorize certain persons to administer the estate of the deceased until it was settled, where the deceased had died intestate, without making a will at all, or leaving a legally invalid will.

In mediaeval times real property, land and certain legally recognized interests in land, usually passed on the death of the holder to his successor by operation of the feudal land law, so that there was little need for any written document setting forth the deceased's wishes about the disposition of his lands or legal interests in land. Similarly, personal property tended to be disposed of by word of mouth or by tacit agreement.

As feudal ties slackened, as population grew and as people's material possessions increased, the need for written dispositions of real and personal property increased, and it became necessary for the authenticity of these documents to be proved before their terms could become effective, and for some court to adjudicate in disputes arising from documents disposing of property. Holding that it was a matter of conscience that the wishes of the deceased should be strictly adhered to and carried out, the church from the 14th century onwards took the role of guardian of the deceased's intentions, and through the ecclesiastical courts exercised jurisdiction in all matters relating to wills and testaments, to the almost total exclusion of lay courts. Hence, until 1858 when probate was removed out of the hands of the church, the proving of almost all wills or the grant of administration of estates of deceased persons who left no wills was carried out in church courts. Certain civil courts established their rights to probate jurisdiction, but these courts were few and their rights, in general, were extremely limited.

The will and the testament, today merged into the one last will and testament, were originally separate documents, performing different functions. The testament was the written disposition of personal property; the will was the written disposition of real property.

According to feudal land law, the disposition of real estate by a will was not possible before 1540. However, the lawyers of the 15th century devised a method of getting around the letter of the law by the development of trusts and uses, so that by the late 15th century the disposition of real estate by will was a commonplace, rules of law notwithstanding. For technical aspects of the subject, the student should read W. S. Holdsworth, *An Historical Introduction to the Land Law* (Oxford, 1927), or any standard work on the English law of land tenure.

The Statute of Wills, 1540, all but abolished the rules which had previously forbidden transfer of land by wills, and allowed the holders of freehold estates to dispose by will of all but a possible small portion of their lands. The abolition of feudal tenures in 1660 removed all restrictions on disposition by will of freehold lands. By the 16th century, convention had devised means to allow even the holder of lands not freehold to make disposition of them by will.

Until the Statute of Frauds of 1667, while a will had to be in writing, it was not necessary for it to be in the testator's writing, nor did it need to be signed by him; after 1667, the written will had to be signed by the testator, in the presence of witnesses, or signed for him at his direction, with direction and signature attested to by credible witnesses.

Ecclesiastical Probate Jurisdiction Before 1858

☼

The Courts of Probate Jurisdiction

ECCLESIASTICAL probate jurisdiction before 1858 is a subject of considerable complexity. Although there are certain broad outlines which could be set forth, they are subject to so many exceptions and anomalies at every stage that they would serve to obscure rather than elucidate the difficulties. It is, therefore, necessary to go into some detail in considering the various courts in which a will might be probated in England and Wales before the reform of 1857.

The easiest way of approaching the problem of ecclesiastical jurisdiction in probate matters is to follow the structure of the Church of England from bottom to top.

The smallest ecclesiastical unit is the parish. The parish was not a unit of probate jurisdiction, except where a single parish or a number of parishes, not necessarily all contiguous, formed an ecclesiastical peculiar, which was a church, or a parish or parishes exempt from the jurisdiction of the diocese in which they lay.

Next in the structure of the church is the rural deanery, frequently abbreviated, unfortunately, in this context to deanery. The rural deanery consists of an unspecified and not constant number of parishes, subject to the authority of a rural dean, normally one of the parochial clergy within the rural deanery. As a rule, rural deaneries were not probate jurisdictions. Within the Diocese of Chester, however, as it existed between its creation in 1541 and 1836, when its area was reduced, certain rural deaneries had probate jurisdiction.

The whole county of Chester, and Lancashire south of the River Ribble, from 1541 to 1847 formed the Archdeaconry of Chester. While the usual practice was the exercise of probate jurisdiction by the Archdeacon, within this Archdeaconry probate jurisdiction was split in two. For estates valued at less than £40, the twelve rural deans exercised jurisdiction within their deaneries, passing on the proved wills and any accompanying documents to the episcopal court of Chester for safekeeping; estates of clergy and esquires valued below £40 were excepted. For estates valued at over £40, together with the estates of clergy and esquires, probate was granted in the episcopal consistory court of the Diocese at Chester. The jurisdictions were known as "infra" and "supra" jurisdictions, and the wills themselves likewise were called "infra" and "supra" wills. The creation of the Diocese of Manchester in 1847 did not affect the Chester jurisdictions in those parts of the old diocese incorporated in the new, and until 1858 Chester was the place of probate and safekeeping of these wills.

Also, in the Diocese of Chester from 1541 to 1836, in the immense Archdeaconry of Richmond which covered Lancashire north of the Ribble, parts of Cumberland and Westmorland, and parts of the North and West Ridings of Yorkshire, grants of probate and administration were made to the eight rural deans under commission from the Commissary of the Archdeacon, and the documents were forwarded to him for retention after probate.

Similarly within the Diocese of York (not the Province) rural deans exercised jurisdiction in probate matters, under commission from the Archbishop as diocesan bishop, for estates solely within the diocese. In these instances the probate jurisdiction of a rural dean cannot be said to be original or *virtute officii.* It was a delegated jurisdiction, exercised on behalf of the person in whom it was originally vested.

Certain other rural deaneries had probate jurisdiction, but these were all peculiar jurisdictions.

Deans of cathedrals frequently exercised probate jurisdiction of a peculiar nature and the term "deanery" is sometimes applied to this. A distinction should always be made between a rural dean and the dean of a cathedral; their offices are distinct and their functions are different, even if their titles are confusingly similar.

The next level in the structure of the church, and in many ways the most important in matters of probate and wills, is the archdeaconry. This is the major subdivision of the diocese, consisting of a number of rural deaneries, and its head is an archdeacon. Before the abolition of the jurisdiction of ecclesiastical courts in probate matters, the archdeacon's court was normally the lowest one in which a will might be proved, or out of which authority to administer an estate might be granted, when the testator had *bona notabilia,* lands or goods worth over £5; no will was necessary for a lesser sum. Except where a parish or group of parishes, or a deanery or deaneries exercised peculiar jurisdiction and were thus exempted from the archdeacon's jurisdiction, and with the exception of the Archdeaconry of Chester, the will of any person having landed estate or personal property entirely within the archdeaconry would normally be proved in the court of the archdeacon. Occasionally, archdeacons did not exercise probate jurisdiction. In these instances the jurisdiction resided in the bishop of the diocese, who would exercise jurisdiction within the archdeaconry through his episcopal consistory court. A case in point is the Archdeaconry of Derby within the Diocese of Lichfield: the archdeacon had no jurisdiction in probate matters, so that the probate of wills which would otherwise have taken place in an archdeacon's court took place in the episcopal consistory court of the Bishop of Lichfield.

From the archdeaconry to the diocese, over which a bishop has control, is the next step in the structure of the church. Through the episcopal consistory court, a diocesan bishop exercised testamentary jurisdiction throughout his diocese, for the probate of wills of persons owning land or having personal property in more than one archdeaconry within the diocese at the time of their death. In such probates the archdeacons' jurisdiction was superseded by that of the bishop. In addition, as the instance of Derby just cited has shown, the diocesan might exercise a sole jurisdiction within a single archdeaconry, when the archdeacon had no jurisdiction. Suffragan bishops exercised no jurisdiction in probate matters simply because they were bishops, but might, if they were also archdeacons, exercise jurisdiction by virtue of being archdeacons. The episcopal court had no jurisdiction over peculiars.

The whole of England and Wales until 1920 was divided ecclesiastically into two provinces: Canterbury, comprising the whole of England south of a line following the southern boundaries of the counties of Cheshire, Yorkshire and Nottingham, and the whole of Wales and the Channel Islands; and York, comprising England north of the boundary specified and including the Isle of Man. Each province was governed by an archbishop. Each archbishop exercised probate jurisdiction within his province with regard to wills concerned with property in more than one diocese or, in theory at least, in more than one peculiar within the province. The two probate courts of the archbishops were called the Prerogative Courts of Canterbury and of York. Just as Canterbury is superior to York in all other ecclesiastical matters, so it was in testamentary matters, since the Archbishop of Canterbury had jurisdiction in the probate of wills concerned with property in both provinces.

The Prerogative Court of Canterbury (more familiarly known by its initials P. C. C., which will be used frequently from this point onwards) was the foremost court of probate in England and Wales before 1858. What gives P. C. C. its primacy in the eyes of genealogists and researchers in the U. S. A. is the fact that this court had jurisdiction for probate of all those with estates in England or Wales who died overseas or at sea. Not, it should be quite clearly understood, probate jurisdiction for all wills made in British possessions, but only over wills of persons dying in the colonies or at sea who left property in England or Wales, whether within one jurisdiction or more. In other words, not all wills made in the colonies were proved in P. C. C., but only those in which the testator left property in England or Wales as well as in the colony in which he lived. Nor had P. C. C. any paramount jurisdiction with regard to wills dealing solely with property in the colonies, but lying in more than one probate jurisdiction overseas. This limitation of the jurisdiction of P. C. C. over wills of persons dying in the colonies is thus strongly emphasized to counter as firmly as possible the mistaken view that all wills of persons dying in Virginia, for example, ought to be found in P. C. C.'s series.

Despite P. C. C.'s paramount jurisdiction in the matter of colonial wills dealing with property in England and Wales, it is not unheard of to find that colonial wills dealing with property lying wholly within the province of York, whether solely within one probate jurisdiction or not, or dealing with property in both provinces, have been proved either in P. C. Y. (Prerogative Court of York) alone, or in P. C. Y. as well as in P. C. C., for greater security and certainty. Occasionally a colonial will proved in P. C. C. or in P. C. Y., or in both, might also be proved in a lower court, if property existed solely within that court's jurisdiction. It is not likely that such a will would be proved solely in the lower court, but odd examples are known.

In a discussion of the position of the archbishops, it should not be forgotten that they were also diocesan bishops of the dioceses of Canterbury and York, within their respective provinces, and that as diocesan bishops they also exercised probate jurisdiction within their dioceses in the same manner as any other diocesan bishop. Thus the episcopal consistory court of Canterbury is the court through which the archbishop exercised his jurisdiction as a diocesan, and this court should not be confused with P. C. C., the court through which he exercised his jurisdiction as archbishop of the province of Canterbury. Similarly, the Archbishop of York exercised diocesan jurisdiction through the episcopal consistory court of York, which must be distinguished from P. C. Y.

Apparent Anomalies in Probate and Administration

In theory, there existed before 1858 an ordered system of courts, in which the probate of wills was granted by ecclesiastical authority. Beginning with archdeaconry (or with rural deanery in the two Chester jurisdictions), the order of courts ran through diocesan and provincial courts to the paramount jurisdiction of P. C. C., exercised throughout England, Wales and the colonies overseas. The theory was more rigid than the practice, however, and it is no uncommon thing to find a will proved in an unexpected court, either for reasons connected with the convenience of executors or administrators of estates, or for unfathomable reasons. But search for a will should always follow the order of the courts, unless some compelling reason exists at the outset to suggest that a course of action different from the one which theory would dictate had been taken in the probate of a will or the administration of an estate.

As a general rule, it may be said that where probate or administration was not granted in the obvious archidiaconal, diocesan or provincial court, then the next step should be to find out if the will was proved in P. C. C. The prestige of this court, the greater security of a probate issued out of P. C. C., and the widespread confidence in its procedures and records as a hedge against possible future litigation, were all reasons why some wills, which it was not essential to prove in P. C. C., were in fact taken to that court for probate. Nor is it unknown for a will to be proved in an inferior court and then to be proved in P. C. C. subsequently.

Theoretically, all ecclesiastical probate courts were subject to breaks in the continuity of business (and hence of records) during the course of visitations by ecclesiastical superiors, the regular visits of inquiry by the bishop or archbishop into ecclesiastical behavior and discipline, or during the interim occurring when the office to which jurisdiction was attached (that of archdeacon, bishop or archbishop) was vacant. These breaks were known as inhibitions and vacancies.

A court was inhibited for a specified period during visitation and jurisdiction might be transferred to the visitant's court (for instance, from archidiaconal court to episcopal court); normally, however, the inhibited court and officials carried on business as usual by virtue of a commission from the visitor, empowering them to function in his name. Hence, although inhibition was a technical reality, in practice neither the business nor the records suffered any hiatus. Where a hiatus in the records of any court does occur for a period of anything from three to nine months, and this can be discovered to coincide with a visitation, then the records of any business transacted in that period should be sought in the archives of the superior jurisdiction.

During a vacancy, jurisdiction was assumed either by the archbishop or by the dean and chapter of the diocese in which jurisdiction lay, but the exercise of the functions of the court by the superior was normally *pro forma* (nominal), as it was usual to reappoint all the officers of the court and authorize it to transact business as before by virtue of a commission. Again, a breach in the records of a court, discovered to be coincident with a vacancy, may be filled by the archives of the superior who had assumed jurisdiction.

The Titles of Ecclesiastical Probate Courts

The titles of ecclesiastical courts having probate jurisdiction may cause some difficulties and confusion, and the following remarks attempt to resolve these or at least reduce them to a minimum. While, in theory, jurisdiction might be vested in a person—archbishop, bishop, archdeacon, rural dean—the exercise of the functions connected with probate was confided to officers, lay or secular, or to a particular court, already exercising other functions under ecclesiastical law, so that in effect probate business would be carried on by a particular, nominated officer.

Thus a bishop would transact probate business through his consistory court; the jurisdiction might be called the bishop's Consistory Court, the Episcopal Consistory, or the Consistorial Court, but these names are all synonyms for a bishop exercising jurisdiction in probate throughout his diocese. As has been noted, there were times where a diocesan bishop, as well as exercising a diocesan jurisdiction, might also exercise a concurrent jurisdiction within an archdeaconry or even, more rarely, within a deanery. This lower jurisdiction was normally identified by some such title as Consistory of the Bishop of Bristol in the Deanery of Bristol, Episcopal Consistory for the Archdeaconry of Chichester, or Commissary of the Bishop of Winchester in the Archdeaconry of Surrey.

Archidiaconal jurisdiction might be exercised through a Commissary or Commissary Court, Consistorial Court or consistory of an archdeaconry (not to be confused with an episcopal commissary or consistory for an archdeaconry), or simply under the title of the archdeaconry, such as Archdeaconry of Berkshire. The distinction between the episcopal court, under whatever title, acting for an archdeaconry or deanery, and the archidiaconal court itself, under a *prima facie* similar title, should be noted carefully, so that record of a will or administration is not sought fruitlessly in the wrong archives.

Courts of Peculiar Jurisdictions

What has been said so far about ecclesiastical jurisdictions in testamentary matters concerns the relatively regular situation in the succession of courts from archdeaconry to P. C. C. Interspersed throughout the two provinces of Canterbury and York were a considerable number of peculiar jurisdictions, which were jurisdictions exempted from the control of the bishop of the diocese within which they lay. It would be impossible within the scope of this Special Report to attempt to explain the historical reasons for the existence of each of these peculiars, although the majority seem to have come into existence at the Reformation and exercised probate jurisdiction until 1858.

Peculiars are of five kinds: royal peculiars, exempt from any jurisdiction save that of the sovereign, like St. Katherine's by the Tower, London; archiepiscopal peculiars, exempt from the control of diocesan bishops and archdeacons, usually places in which the archbishops had extensive possessions, such as the thirteen parishes in the City of London, which formed the peculiar administered by the Dean of Arches on behalf of the Archbishop of Canterbury; episcopal peculiars in other dioceses, exempt from the control of the bishops in whose dioceses they lay (few if any of this class of peculiar had probate jurisdiction); peculiars of bishops in their own dioceses exempt from archidiaconal control (again, few had separate probate jurisdiction); and peculiars of deans (and deans and chapters) of cathedrals, prebends (places where special sums of money or grants of land were once given to a cathedral church for the maintenance of a priest in the cathedral, the prebend being named after the place), cathedral officers, and individual parishes over which the diocesan bishop had surrendered control (this is by far the most numerous category of peculiars with probate jurisdiction).

Peculiars might comprise no more than a single parish, but were usually a group of parishes, not necessarily contiguous or geographically compact, occasionally exempt from archiepiscopal control, but usually outside only the control of the diocesan bishop. Probate of wills within a peculiar was the prerogative of the holder of the office or the body to whom the peculiar belonged. It should be noted here that deans of cathedrals, especially of pre-Reformation cathedrals, usually had a probate jurisdiction, which should not be confused with the jurisdiction exercised by a rural dean as in the Diocese of Chester, nor with an archiepiscopal peculiar jurisdiction within a rural deanery, nor with an episcopal jurisdiction within a rural deanery.

As with the more regular jurisdictions, peculiars were subject to inhibition and vacancy, though not with such regularity of pattern. Where inhibition and vacancy occurred, the same procedures as have been outlined earlier made possible the continued transaction of business and continuity of records: a superior might exercise jurisdiction in fact, and records for the period of the hiatus may be found in the archives of the superior, or jurisdiction might be exercised *pro forma* by commission and no hiatus occur.

Secular Probate Jurisdiction Before 1858

¤

Although probate was primarily an ecclesiastical matter before the Court of Probate Act, 1857, became operative on 1 January 1858, it was not exclusively so. Certain secular corporations or other bodies exercised probate jurisdiction within the boundaries of their respective territories, and this aspect of probate jurisdiction should not be neglected. Indeed, in 1653 Parliament removed testamentary jurisdiction entirely from ecclesiastical courts and vested it in a secular commission, sitting in London and exercising jurisdiction throughout England and Wales. This was, in effect, P. C. C. in lay dress; the records of this commission are now a part of the records of P. C. C., so that continuity over the centuries is preserved in one series. The jurisdiction of P. C. C. was restored to that court when Charles II came to the throne in 1660.

It is not, however, unusual to find wills bearing dates between 1642 and 1660 in the records of lower ecclesiastical jurisdictions; these are normally found to be registrations effected after 1660 and antedated, or reregistrations of original London probates under the date of the original. It is, therefore, advisable when one is searching for a will presumed to have been probated during the Civil War, and not found in P. C. C. records, to check with the records of any lower jurisdiction in which the testator may be known or reasonably presumed to have had goods and lands.

The Chancellors of the Universities of Oxford and Cambridge had probate jurisdiction for persons who had matriculated in the universities and were in residence as members of a university, or of a college, at the time of their death. In view of the preponderantly ecclesiastical nature of the universities until the 18th century, there might be some justification for regarding these courts as quasi-ecclesiastical in nature. However, being subject to no ecclesiastical oversight, they are more properly to be considered secular.

The Court of Hustings of the Corporation of London is frequently said to have been a court of probate but never, in fact, was. Wills are enrolled on the rolls of this court when they deal with property within the City of London, but such enrollment is simply to give public testimony to the will and to enable title to property to be proved by reference to the rolls at a later date, if it should prove necessary. In other municipal corporations, Bristol and Exeter for example, wills were frequently recorded in a similar manner, but here again recording is not synonymous with probate.

It is believed that one or two corporations, such as Higham Ferrars in Northamptonshire and Kings Lynn in Norfolk, did exercise limited probate jurisdiction within the borough boundaries; but how far such jurisdictions were exclusive of any ecclesiastical jurisdiction, and how far a prior probate in an ecclesiastical court was essential to the validity of such wills, is a matter which would require much research.

The most numerous type of secular jurisdiction was that enjoyed by courts of manors or groups of manors (known as honors) which had jurisdiction over wills relating to lands exclusively within their boundaries. Many such jurisdictions might be ecclesiastical in origin, that is to say originally the property of an ecclesiastic with a peculiar jurisdiction, but on transfer, by sale or gift, to a layman, the probate powers of the court became vested in secular hands. Some of these courts are understood to have claimed the right to prove wills of persons who died within their boundaries regardless of the situation of the property of the deceased. How far such claims were pressed and how far they were merely formal is not clear, but it is believed that formality and not actuality was the case. The record of probates granted by such courts might be found in the court rolls of the manors, but more usually separate series of probate records were kept.

Finally, the royal peculiars, mentioned for convenience under the general remarks on peculiars in the section on ecclesiastical probate jurisdictions, might be mentioned here as more proper to be thought of as secular than as ecclesiastical in nature.

The introductory account of probate jurisdiction has been stated in general terms in order to cover the field as adequately as possible without excessive detail. No attempt has been made to give an historical account of how the various ecclesiastical courts came into being nor of how they worked; their operation in probate matters will be considered later in this Special Report. A valuable account of ecclesiastical courts, one of the most comprehensive available within one cover, is to be found in the *Report of the Royal Commission on Ecclesiastical Courts* (Command Paper C37601 of 1883). Another general account will be found in Felix Makower, *The Constitutional History and Constitution of the Church of England* (London, 1895). More detailed accounts for the provinces of Canterbury and York are contained in B. L. Woodcock, *Medieval Ecclesiastical Courts in the Diocese of Canterbury* (London, 1952), and C. I. A. Ritchie, *The Ecclesiastical Courts of York* (Arbroath, 1956). For some account of the practices of church courts, Richard Burn, *The Ecclesiastical Law* (9th edition, London, 1842) and R. J. Phillimore, *The Ecclesiastical Law of the Church of England* (2nd edition, London, 1895) may be consulted. All these works include more than probate matters, but are useful in showing the background of the history of ecclesiastical courts and in putting probate jurisdiction in perspective.

The 1882 Royal Commission was not the first 19th century inquiry into the workings and jurisdiction of ecclesiastical courts. From 1827 onwards a series of parliamentary papers were published by authority of the House of Commons, giving detailed returns of all courts, ecclesiastical and secular, which dealt with probate of wills, setting out the extent of their jurisdictions and any inhibitions to which they were subject, stating where and by whom the records were kept, the extent of the records and their condition, and giving lists of fees charged for inspection and copying of wills and other fees.

Despite their age these returns are extremely valuable for the information they give about jurisdictions, inhibitions and extent of the records. The other matters with which they were concerned are now of little more than academic interest, since recent arrangements for custody of pre-1858 wills bear no relation to the position in the 1830's. These returns have formed the basis for a number of hitherto standard books on wills. The principal Parliamentary Papers concerned are: Nos. 372 of 1828; 177 of 1829 (fuller than and superseding that of 1828); 205 of 1830 (valuable for lists of records then extant); 199 of 1832 (which may be cited as of considerable value for its exposition of the canon law in relation to probate). Certain other papers were issued which do not seem to add materially to those listed above. These papers of 1828-1832 are very useful for the information they contain on the subject generally. Perhaps more readily available and no less valuable are the returns of records held by some of the ecclesiastical courts, especially P. C. C., printed as appendices to the *Report of the Commissioners Appointed to Inquire into the State of the Public Records* (London, 1837). These returns are obviously based on the 1832 return previously mentioned. As a matter of interest, the *Report of the Royal Commission on Public Records* (London, 1912-1919) might be compared with the 1837 report as an indication of what changes had come about in the keeping and availability of the probate records. All these 19th century reports and returns are admittedly of mainly academic interest, but they should not be ignored on that account.

B. G. Bouwens, *Wills and their Whereabouts* (London, 1939), is most frequently cited as an essential reference book in research involving probate matters. A second edition, with a list of new places of deposit of certain groups of probate records, by Miss H. G. Thacker, was issued by the Society of Genealogists in 1950. This second edition contains no amendments to Bouwens' original text. The principal value of Bouwens' book is the detailed account it gives of jurisdictions, inhibitions, the extent of records as of 1939, and occasional explanatory notes. Anthony J. Camp, *Wills and Their Whereabouts* (Canterbury, 1963), completely supersedes Bouwens' book as to the location of probate records. Camp brings up to date extensive transfers from the secular probate registries to county record offices and other archive depositories. An appendix to this Special Report gives the current position as to whereabouts. Relisting by the repositories concerned will doubtless have improved on Bouwens' account of the extent of the records, and it has added considerably to the information on the contents of the various series which they hold. The details available in Felix Hull, ed., *Guide to the Kent County Archives Office* (Maidstone, 1958), pp. 107-123, should be compared with those in Bouwens' book. Guides to the Bedford and Sussex record offices contain similar lists. Unpublished lists are available in such repositories as now hold probate records, and can be consulted at those repositories.

Probate Jurisdiction After 1858

¤

By the Court of Probate Act, 1857 (20 and 21 Victoria, cap. 77), the probate of wills was taken out of the hands of the church and vested in a secular court, known today as the Probate, Divorce and Admiralty Division of the Supreme Court of Judicature, the additional responsibilities being added to the court by subsequent legislation. However, wills and administrations of persons dying in Jersey continued to be proved in the court of the Dean of Jersey, who retained his jurisdiction until 1949. In that year a new constitution of the island transferred the jurisdiction to the Royal Court of Jersey.

Under the terms of the 1857 Act, England and Wales were divided into civil probate districts with one Principal Probate Registry in London, now and for many years past at Somerset House, Strand, London, W. C. 2. In each probate district, one town (usually the diocesan seat, but not always so) has a district probate registry, in which wills of persons dying within the district are proved, or letters of administration of the estate are granted. A copy of each will proved and every administration granted by the district registries is sent to the Principal Probate Registry, where an annual master index is kept. It is true that all English and Welsh wills after 1858 can be found at Somerset House.

Access to these later wills is governed by orders made by the President of the Probate, Divorce and Admiralty Division (the senior judge of the court) under statutory authority, and subject to variation from time to time.

It is improbable that American searchers will have much need to search wills of later date than 1858 for genealogical reasons, although occasions may arise. However, probate records since 1858 are relatively straightforward, and a letter to the Principal Probate Registry stating the relevant details of the will it is hoped to find will be sure to bring a reply.

The Proving of a Will Before 1858

☼

It is the intention of this section of the Report to consider the steps taken, theoretically, in the probate of a will, or granting of letters of administration in cases of intestacy. The section will define terms frequently met with in dealing with probate records, explain the general pattern of records, and give guidance on what to expect from probate records generally. The theoretical aspect of this account should be emphasized, as practices varied from place to place and what is true of one court may not necessarily be true of any other. A special section dealing with the records of the Prerogative Court of Canterbury follows later in this report.

As soon as possible after the death of the person whose will it was intended to submit for probate, the executors named in the will, or their duly authorized legal agent, took the original will (or occasionally a notarized copy, if the testator died abroad) to the appropriate court or officer duly empowered to handle probate matters on behalf of the court, for scrutiny. On being satisfied of the authenticity of the document and of the testator's power to make a valid will, the court or officer would prove the will and make it legally valid by passing a probate act. This act might be recorded in a separate Probate Act Book and also, in some courts, endorsed on the original will; certainly one or other procedure would be followed, if not both. Some courts required executors to enter into a testamentary bond, by which they were bound in a sum of money to "well and faithfully" carry out the terms of the will.

Having passed the probate act and recorded it in some way, the court or officer would then make a probate copy of the will, annex it to letters of probate (a copy of the probate act) and seal the two documents together, handing them to the executors as their authority to carry out the terms of the will. The original will would be retained by the court to be kept in the series of filed wills. Frequently another copy was entered in a bound volume or register of registered wills, which could be consulted by interested persons and be easily available for office use. Registered wills usually have a copy of the probate act immediately beneath them. This practice of retaining the original will and returning the probate copy to the executors is almost universal after 1660; before 1660, it would appear that some courts did the reverse—returned the original and kept the probate copy—but still maintained the series of registered wills. Registration was usually made only after payment of a fee for the service; since some executors could not or would not pay this, in most courts among the filed wills can be found unregistered wills, which do not appear in the registers, but are none the less legally valid. They may be filed in series with the filed wills or as a separate series; they should not be confused with unproved wills, of which copies or series may exist in some courts. Probate Act Books were usually compiled from day to day, as acts were made, and registered wills were usually copied into the registers in the same way, though variations exist from court to court. Where a testamentary bond was issued, a counterpart is usually to be found with the filed will.

When one executor was a minor at the time of probate, the probate act would grant probate to the other executor, reserving the right of the minor to apply for and receive a probate act and letters of probate when he attained his majority. Some courts made this an occasion for second or double probate of a will, which might mean reregistration or, more usually, a marginal annotation of the facts on the registered will. When both executors were minors, the court would issue letters of curation and a curation bond to a named guardian or guardians, if the children were under the age of fourteen, or letters of tuition and a tuition bond, if the children were between fourteen and twenty-one. These bonds authorized the person or persons named to act on the children's behalf until their majority, when they could act on their own behalf. Curation and tuition documents are usually found together with the filed will; and mention of a grant of curation or tuition will usually be found entered in the Probate Act Book.

On occasions, executors renounced their right to act and entered a renunciation, again usually with the filed will, and often entered in the Probate Act Book. If both executors entered renunciations (or if both died), the court made other arrangements for administration of the estate. This was normally done by appointing next of kin of the testator as administrator, and issuing to him (or them) letters of administration with will annexed (that is, a copy of the will and original probate act).

Where a person was on the point of death and no written will had been made, a nuncupative will could be made: the testator declared his wishes verbally before credible witnesses, who wrote them down. This nuncupative will, together with depositions as to its authenticity (sworn before the court or some person duly authorized to take such depositions), was entered and probate in the usual manner followed. Except for persons on active service in war, nuncupative wills were barred after 1838.

In instances of intestacy, when no will was known to exist or when none could be found, the next of kin, in person or by duly appointed legal agent, applied to the probate court for letters of administration of the estate. The steps were the same as for probate. The court would issue an administration act, register it in an Administration Act Book and give letters of administration to the person seeking them, who would at the same time enter into an administration bond.

In early days all courts, before granting probate or administration, required the executors to file an inventory of the goods of the testator: in this task the executors were helped by an overseer or supervisor, normally named in the will. Inventories are usually to be found with filed wills. In some courts, especially P. C. C., inventories soon ceased to be required; in others, as in the Chester courts, they continued to be required up to 1858.

Where there was a dispute over a will and the court which was asked to grant probate heard the cases of both sides (or more accurately, read the cases, since most ecclesiastical procedure was by written rather than oral testimony), it would give verdict; and if probate was granted, this was done by sentence, not probate act. The papers in the case will almost certainly be found in the judicial papers of the court concerned, and will not be with the probate records. The original will is almost sure to be with the case papers. These may not always be in the same repository as the probate records of the court. While no filed will may be found, a registered will can be expected in the register. Wills proved by sentence are often, and especially in P. C. C., to be found in manuscript indexes not under the testator's name, but under a general head Sentences or Sententiae.

In order to find wills and administrations needed for office business, the officials of probate courts maintained manuscript indexes in volume form, usually called Calendars. These were normally alphabetical and in such form serve as indexes to the records, but their defects should always be kept in mind. The Calendar, prepared by officials of the court in the course of carrying out business, should be distinguished from any subsequent index, manuscript or printed, which may have been prepared. In general, a later index arranged alphabetically and compiled from both filed and registered wills may be considered superior to the Calendar, which may have been compiled only from the registers, and not necessarily alphabetically. Where no later or printed index exists, then naturally the Calendar is the sole finding aid.

It may be appropriate here to draw attention to the fact that wills exist in many archive and manuscript repositories which are not necessarily a part of the archives of a probate court. Every collection of family papers contains original wills (proved or not), draft wills, probate copies with letters of probate annexed, office copies made by solicitors in their handling of estates and other copies. Such wills are a part of the family archive or manuscript collection in which they are found, not a part of the archives of a probate court. Similarly, many wills are found copied into the minute books of municipal corporations, into parish registers, and even into special volumes of wills, as reference copies for the officers of the institutions concerned which are beneficiaries under the terms of the will. The purpose of such copies, especially in municipal records, may be misunderstood to the extent that it is thought that the corporation had probate jurisdiction.

In manorial and prebendal jurisdictions, filed wills, as well as administrations in intestacy, and subsidiary documents, may still survive, but not necessarily registers, since the extent and frequency of operation of jurisdiction may not have warranted their upkeep. In manorial jurisdictions, registration may have been effected on the court rolls of the manor, not now surviving.

The Prerogative Court of Canterbury and Its Records

☼

As this court is the one in which wills of Virginians having *bona notabilia* in England and Wales are most likely to be found, a fuller discussion of its records now follows. The records of the Prerogative Court of York, in which Virginian wills of persons having *bona notabilia* solely within the Province of York may be found, are neither so well known nor so readily available as those of Canterbury, unfortunately, but some account of these records is also included in this Special Report.

As might be expected in a court exercising so wide a jurisdiction as P. C. C., business became departmentalized: five sections, or Seats as they were called, dealt with the various wills brought to the court for probate or with the issue of letters of administration for estates within the geographical area for which each seat was responsible. The Seats were these:

Name of Seat	*Area Covered*
Registers Seat	The Province of York, and parts overseas (foreign parts).
Surrey Seat	Counties of Cornwall, Devon, Somerset, Dorset, Wiltshire, Surrey and Sussex.
Welsh Seat	Wales and Monmouthshire, and the counties of Shropshire, Stafford, Derby, Hereford, Worcester, Warwick, Leicester, Rutland, Northampton, Gloucester, Oxford and Berkshire.
Middlesex Seat	Counties of Bedford, Buckingham, Cambridge, Essex, Hertford, Huntingdon, Kent, Lincoln, Norfolk, Suffolk, and Middlesex, including St. Paul, Covent Garden; St. Martin in the Fields; St. Dunstan,

	Stepney; St. Clement Dane; St. Paul, Shadwell; and other parishes in the outparts of Middlesex.
LONDON SEAT	The City of London and its suburbs, but excluding any in the Middlesex Seat above.

As far as the Calendars of wills, filed wills and registered wills are concerned, the five seats have no significance. The Probate and Administration Act Books of the Court, however, are affected by the seats in that the acts, in order of being granted, are arranged in order of seats, Registers Seat preceding the others. The seats are not identified by geographical name, but by a personal name, presumably that of one of the officials of the section, or possibly by the surname of the person whose estate is concerned in the first grant in each volume. Provided, therefore, that one knows the place of residence of a deceased person, the probate or administration act can be found in the Act Books more speedily than otherwise. The Act Books for Registers Seat will always have to be searched for Virginian entries.

The registers of wills are the great glory of P. C. C. and the series of records most frequently consulted by searchers in the Literary Search Department at the Principal Probate Registry at Somerset House. In P. C. C., as in other courts, from earliest time it was the usual practice to copy a will, once proved, into a register for ease of future reference and consultation. There are more than 2,200 square folio volumes containing registered copies of wills proved in the court between 1383 and 1858. As these are the most frequently consulted records, they merit some detailed consideration.

Before 1841, these registers are not identified by year, but by a name. A register is not necessarily synonymous with a volume, since very often a single register comprises several volumes, all referred to by the same name and continuously foliated. Before about 1550 a register might cover several years of registration; after about 1550, it was usual to have only one register for each year. Down to 1572, the registers are called by the surname of the person whose will is first in the book, with the exception of the register Crumwell for 1536-1540; this register takes its name from Thomas Cromwell, Henry VIII's Vicar-General. (Its contents seem to indicate that Cromwell exercised a testamentary jurisdiction independently of P. C. C., but apparently without effect on the validity of the wills registered.) From 1572 to 1650, it was usual to put the will of some person of prominence—peer, knight, important officer of P. C. C.—as the first will registered and to call the volume after him. From 1651 to 1840, the name given to a register was chosen arbitrarily from the volume and was normally that of some one of national prominence: the register for 1804 is Pitt, and that for 1805 is Nelson. From 1841 to 1858, registers are identified by year only. Lists of the registers, chronologically and alphabetically arranged, are printed in J. Challenor C. Smith, comp., *Index of Wills Proved in the Prerogative Court of Canterbury, 1383-1558* . . . (London, 1893-1895): Index Library, Vols. X-XI, 2 vols. The lists were first printed in *The New-England Historical and Genealogical Register,* Vol. XLVI (July 1892), pp. 299-302. Copies of the lists are displayed in the Literary Search Department at the Principal Probate Registry.

The registers are not numbered by pages, nor by folios in the usual sense (one sheet with a *recto* and *verso* bearing one number), but are foliated in a special fashion. Each gathering or quire of leaves is called a folio and may consist of sixteen or more pages. Each register, whether a single volume or several under one name, is foliated in this way, continuously. Reference to registered wills in printed volumes is normally in the following form: P. C. C. Rous 123. This means Prerogative Court of Canterbury, register called Rous, folio 123; the f. (for folio) used in citing records foliated in the more normal manner is usually omitted in P. C. C. citations. Thus in searching for a will in Rous 123, folio 123 has to be found and the pages within the folio searched until the required will is discovered. The probate act is normally recorded along with the will.

Most of the time the registered will is all the searcher needs to consult, and provided he has obtained the necessary permit from the Principal Probate Registry, he may consult the registers free of charge. If an original will was not registered but the original or a probate copy is among the filed wills, then the filed will is produced without fee.

The series of registers is unbroken from 1383; the series of original or probate copy wills is less complete for the obvious reason that one will is more easily lost than one register. Between 1484 and 1524 original wills are rare; from 1524 to 1620 they are much more frequent; from 1620 to 1858 virtually none are missing. Bouwens (p. 48) gives a brief list of the gaps in the series; House of Commons Paper 205 of 1830 and the 1837 Report of the Record Commission both give a detailed list of bundles of wills for each month of each year. In the printed indexes of P. C. C. wills, to be mentioned more fully later, the existence of a filed will corresponding to a registered will is denoted by the letter F before the register and folio reference up to about 1580; thereafter the existence of a registered will is usually held to denote existence of a filed will. The practice of P. C. C., common till the end of the 16th century, of keeping the probate copy on file and returning the original to the executors, has previously been mentioned and should be borne in mind when filed wills are asked for, as an explanation of why an "original" original is not forthcoming.

Probate Act Books, the volumes in which the probate acts were registered, exist for the years 1526 to 1858, except for 1538-1548, 1550, 1553, 1554 and 1662. Since the act is normally copied into the register with the will, it is not likely to be necessary to consult the Act Books very often. Where filed wills are consulted and the act is not endorsed on the original, it may be necessary to consult the Act Books if evidence of probate of the will is required.

On occasion Probate Act Books may give information of genealogical value not to be found in the registered or filed will. They give the place of death of the testator and possibly places where he resided during his life, which could be important for Virginians who came back to England and died there; or, alternatively, they might provide or suggest the place of origin of persons who settled in Virginia and left no certain evidence of their English origins. Being compiled from day to day, the Probate Act Books usually form a more complete index to the wills than do the manuscript calendars. It might well be worth the additional labor involved in any work done on P. C. C. wills of Virginians to check the Probate and Administration Act Books in case any extra worthwhile information appears in them. Only the volumes for Registers Seat need be searched for entries relating to persons dying in Virginia and leaving estate in England and Wales.

Bouwens' book and earlier books dealing with P. C. C. records mention the series of inventories accompanying wills, which were at one time kept in the Principal Probate Registry. These were destroyed by a bomb which fell on Somerset House during the Second World War. References in any prewar book on P. C. C. wills to their extent and possible interest can now have no more than historical interest.

When a person died intestate the court would issue letters of administration, usually to the next of kin, record the action of issuing the letters in the Administration Act Book, and require the administrators to enter into a bond for administering the estate properly. A complete series of Administration Act Books exists for the years 1559 to 1858, except for the year 1662. A separately filed series of bonds exists virtually complete for the years 1730 to 1858, with some for the period 1714 to 1730; these are, however, not at present available for inspection by the public. For information on grants of administration for estates of Virginians, a search of the Administration Act Books would seem to be essential in view of the detail that may be recorded therein, and not be available elsewhere. As with Probate Act Books, so with Administration Act Books, the Registers Seat is the series to be searched for grants of administration of estate in England and Wales.

For wills, registered or filed, and for administrations (usually abbreviated to admons) there is a series of manuscript Calendars or indexes at the Principal Probate Registry. These Calendars are indexes to both wills and administrations for the period covered by each volume. From 1654 onwards, the Calendars are usually for one year only; before that, one Calendar might cover a span of years.

The Calendar lists the name of testator or intestate, the county (or occasionally the town) of residence, or for persons dying overseas, merely the word Parts, abbreviated to Pts. For wills there is a reference to the folio of the register concerned, but for administrations merely a reference to the month in which the letters of administration were granted.

The arrangement of the Calendars is irregular and inconsistent. Names are entered under the initial letter of the name of testator or intestate, but names beginning with the same letter are not in alphabetical order under that letter. In some Calendars, the index to wills is in one column of a page with the index to administrations in the adjoining column. Sometimes all wills under a letter are listed together, with all administrations under that letter listed below. Sometimes all wills for the year covered by a particular Calendar are indexed by letter, then separately and afterwards all administrations for that year are indexed.

For reasons to be explained shortly, reference to these Calendars for all wills and some administrations before 1701 is not necessary. Care should be taken in using the Calendars after 1700, since any probate granted, after trial in P. C. C., by sentence of the court may be indexed under S for Sentence and not under the initial letter of the testator's surname. This pitfall is common until well into the 18th century; later the indexing of probates after sentence was under the surname initial of the testator. In any case, details of the sentence pronounced by the court will usually be found entered at the end of the last volume of each named register, before 1841, or numbered register, after 1841.

Certain other peculiarities of P. C. C. Calendars may be usefully noted here in explanation and as a safeguard against incorrect interpretation:

(1) In the part of the Calendar relating to administrations, the entry "admon with will annexed" or "admon d.b.n." (an abbreviation for *de bonis non administratis,* with goods not administered) means that the deceased left a legally valid will but, for one of many reasons, the executors did not act. The court therefore granted letters of administration with will annexed to next of kin or others to administer the terms of the will. The will is neither registered nor filed; it is with the original administration records, not at present available for inspection.

(2) On occasions, a will was the subject of a later grant of probate (second or double probate) and for these the Calendar entry will give a reference back to the register and folio at which the first grant and registered copy of the will may be found; similarly a second grant of administration will carry a reference back to

the first grant of administration. The will would not be registered a second time, but merely the probate act.

(3) The words "Limited Probate" are sometimes found in the Calendars of wills as are "Limited Administration" in the Calendars of administrations. These relate to probate or administration, under P. C. C. jurisdiction, of certain limited portions of a deceased person's estate. For the years 1781, 1800, 1802 and 1806-1858, there is a special series of Limited Probate Books, in which are set out full details of such limited probates as were granted in those years. There is a similar series of Limited Administration Books for 1815-1858. For the periods for which these two special series do not exist, full details of the limitations of probate or administration are entered in the Probate or Administration Act Book for the year or period concerned. Limited probates or administrations are frequently connected with people dying abroad with property within the jurisdiction of P. C. C., who had appointed separate executors for this property; in such instances, P. C. C. would grant to these separate executors probate limited to that part of the estate for which the testator wished them to act. In the register Taverner for 1772 at folio 263 is entered the will of John Morton Jordan of Annapolis, Maryland, of which P. C. C. granted limited probate relating to Jordan's English estate only. The full details of the proceedings leading to this grant are entered in the Probate Act Book for 1772.

(4) If the letters N. B. are used to indicate the place of residence of a person mentioned in the Calendar, that person resided in Scotland.

(5) Entries in the Calendars for soldiers usually give their regiments, and for seamen, naval or merchant marine, the names of their ships. The name of a ship should not always be held to indicate a seaman, for many emigrants from England in the 17th century at least described themselves as of a certain ship, since they had no more permanent place of residence.

In searching for wills before 1701, the student is well served by printed indexes and abstracts published in the British Record Society's *Index Library* or in a few individual volumes not part of that series. These printed indexes are far superior to the manuscript calendars in their accuracy, their numerical content and the information they give, to such an extent that the manuscript calendars up to and including 1700 may be ignored. The manuscript calendars for wills give no more than surname, Christian names, county or city of residence or merely Pts (for Parts overseas), and folio reference to the register. But where index and register cover the same period or register name and folio, and where index and registers may not coincide, the printed indexes give the surname, Christian name, status or profession and the exact place of residence, together with register and folio reference. Moreover, being compiled from registers of wills, filed wills and Probate Act Books, the printed indexes include many references not in the Calendars and increase considerably both the number of wills made available and ease of reference to them. For example, whereas it is necessary to look at the will to find out if a will after 1700 with the Calendar reference Pts relates to a Virginian, the printed indexes indicate if the testator's will says he is of Virginia. What the indexes will not tell the searcher is whether the will of a testator living elsewhere in America than in Virginia during his life time deals with property or persons in Virginia. These facts could be discovered only by looking at the will. It should not be forgotten that probate of a Virginian's will in P. C. C. may occur well after 1783 if he had *bona notabilia* in England. The year 1783 does not mark the end of probate of American wills in P. C. C.

It ought perhaps to be emphasized that neither the manuscript Calendars nor the printed indexes give any indication of the contents of the will, the bequests it makes, the property with which it is concerned, or the family relationships of beneficiaries. They are solely indexes to testators, so that while it is easy to discover from the printed indexes whether a testator resided in Virginia, and less easy to discover this fact from the Calendars, neither will disclose whether a testator resident in England at the time of his death mentioned Virginia, Virginian property or Virginian kin in his will, or had any connection with the colony at all. Rare exceptions do occur of persons having a Virginian connection, not disclosed in their statement of place of residence, and these can be found in the printed indexes but not in the Calendars. But these exceptions do not vitiate the general principle just stated. Thus, only the searcher's specialized knowledge, or rational guess or pure hunch will serve to identify testators dying in England, whose wills will have, or may be reasonably presumed to have, a Virginian interest.

Printed indexes to administrations, based on the Calendars and Administration Act Books, are not as numerous as indexes to the wills, but indexes for 1559-1595, 1620-1630 and 1649-1660 have been published. Their accuracy and coverage are greater than those of the Calendars and they should be used in preference to the Calendars. The information these printed indexes give on administrations is similar to that given in printed indexes to wills.

Access to the records of P. C. C. at the Literary Search Department, Principal Probate Registry, Somerset House, Strand, London, W. C. 2, is easy provided the first formalities are observed. Anyone wishing to search the records should apply in writing to the President of the Probate, Divorce and Admiralty Division at the Principal Probate Registry, marking the envelope "Department for Literary Inquiry." The letter, stating the applicant's name, address, profession or status and object of research clearly described, should be accompanied by some certificate stating that the applicant is a proper person to whom the privilege may be granted. Application in person may be made in cases of urgency but it is preferable to obtain permission by writing before visiting the Registry. A permit authorized by the President of the Division is issued once the application is approved and gives the applicant free admission to the Literary Search Department for one year. The recipient must sign the permit on receipt and it is personal to the holder and is not transferable. Breach of the regulations, to be mentioned below, renders the permit liable to forfeiture.

Each searcher must sign the attendance register on arrival. Searchers may inspect without fee the Calendar of wills proved and administrations granted and read the registered copies of the wills, Probate and Administration Act Books. All P. C. C. records up to and including 1858 in these categories are now available for consultation. No copy of all or part of a document may be made except with permission, only an abstract of the whole or a part. No tracing may be made and no ink used in making abstracts. No more than two register books at a time will be produced for one searcher and no more than eight in a day, except by special arrangement. Production of filed wills is made only by previous appointment and for each such document produced a fee of one shilling is chargeable. It is possible that if for some special purpose a considerable number of filed wills is required, some special arrangements over fees might be arrived at, but this statement is not made with any official sanction. As was noted above, a filed will is produced without fee if an original will was not registered but the original or a probate copy is among the filed wills. Abstracts of a whole or part of a filed will may be made free of charge; a copy of all or part may be made only on payment of a further fee in accordance with a statutory scale which varies according to the number of words copied. Negative photostat copies of entries in the registers or Act Books and of filed wills can be supplied at the rate of two shillings per foolscap page.

The Research Department of the Genealogical Society of the Church of Jesus Christ of the Latter Day Saints (the Mormons) in Salt Lake City, Utah, holds microfilms of the whole of the P. C. C. registers of wills and of such filed wills as have no registered counterpart. The availability of these microfilms and the conditions under which they may be inspected should be ascertained from the Society. It should be emphasized that the filed original will has been microfilmed only when no copy of the will has been entered in a register. Many original wills of Virginians or of Virginian interest or connection in P. C. C. must, therefore, not have been microfilmed. The same is true of original wills in P. C. C. of testators in other parts of the U. S. A.

Many English and American record and genealogical societies and individual scholars have printed abstracts or full texts of P. C. C. wills relating to their own areas or to their own particular fields of interest. Such volumes must be taken at their face value and should not be thought to supersede in any way the printed indexes. The method of and motive for printing wills in these volumes should always be ascertained from the compiler's introduction or preface. The selection of wills made by H. F. Waters, *Genealogical Gleanings in England* (Boston, 1901) may be cited as one example of such work.

The Court of Delegates

☼

THE Court of Delegates was not a court of probate, but one with probate appellate jurisdiction. It was set up by Act of Parliament in 1533 as a court of appeal from the Prerogative Courts of Canterbury and York and from Irish probate courts, with some other functions. It was not a court in continuous session but was convened as occasion required to hear cases in probate matters on appeal from any of the courts just mentioned. If the court found in favor of the will, it would by decree enter sentence that probate be granted in the court from which the appeal came. Thus, in P. C. C., the will would normally be registered after the probate act was issued, but, until the 18th century, indexed in the Calendars under Sentence.

Muniment Books of the Court are in the Principal Probate Registry and many copies of wills are entered in them. An index to the wills in these volumes is to be found in *The Genealogist* (New Series, Vol. XI, pp. 165-171, 224-227; Vol. XII, pp. 97-101). Microfilm of the Muniment Books is in the Research Department of the Genealogical Society of the Mormon Church.

The other records of the Court of Delegates are to be found in the Public Record Office, Chancery Lane, London, W. C. 2, where they may be inspected. A brief description of these records is contained in *A Guide to the Manuscripts Preserved in the Public Record Office* (London, 1963), Volume I, pp. 163-164. These records may provide valuable supplementary information on Virginian wills proved after sentence of the court, and a search for the relevant records in the archives of the court would be worthwhile.

The Court of Delegates was abolished in 1832, and its functions were exercised between then and 1858 by the Judicial Committee of the Privy Council, in whose records later documents relating to probate appeals are to be found.

The Prerogative Court of York and Its Records

¤

York tends in probate matters to be overshadowed by Canterbury. The registers of wills for the Prerogative Court of York, which appears to have exercised some form of concurrent jurisdiction with the Exchequer Court of the Diocese of York, number only some 246 volumes as against P. C. C. 's 2,200.

Theoretically, the wills of persons dying with estates within two dioceses or two peculiars within the Province of York were supposed to be proved in P. C. Y., or grants of administration of the estates of intestates granted out of this court. In so far as the estates of persons dying outside England and Wales are concerned, probate in P. C. Y. was theoretically necessary in similar cases. The extent to which theory and practice coincided can only be tested for Virginian examples by a search of the printed indexes to the court's records, for 1389-1688. Certainly examples could be found, but it is thought that generally P. C. C. was the usual court of probate for wills of persons dying in parts overseas leaving *bona notabilia* in England, and thus requiring English probate for the validity of bequests affecting such property. While there is every likelihood that wills of Virginian value should be found at York, they are by no means likely to rival in number those known to exist in the records of P. C. C. For this reason, and also because less is known and generally available about the York records, the account of P. C. Y. records is much less detailed than that for P. C. C.

The general pattern of P. C. Y. records is the same as that for P. C. C. and the procedures and steps in obtaining grant of probate or administration similar. From 1559, the original will was retained by the court and kept in the series of filed wills. A few wills exist for the period 1559-1596; the series is fuller for 1599-1652, though there are none for 1614 and 1624; and from 1660 to 1858 the file is virtually complete, though there are no wills for 1696. The Probate Act Books, in which the probate acts are entered, are complete, and cover the years 1502-1652 and 1660-1858. It will be noticed that between 1652 and 1660 P. C. Y.'s jurisdiction was completely ousted by the lay successor of P. C. C. operating in London. The registered copies of the wills are to be found in 246 volumes covering the periods 1389-1637, 1660-1684, 1688-1690, 1697-1699, and 1705-1858. There is no naming of registers in P. C. Y. as in P. C. C., the volumes being identified by date and a serial numeration. Foliation, as far as is known, is normal and not after the P. C. C. fashion.

There are manuscript Calendars to the registered wills and to administrations for 1389-1688 and 1731-1858. The earlier series of Calendars are superseded by printed indexes to wills in the York Registry published in the Record Series of the Yorkshire Archaeological Society. These indexes also deal, as their titles would indicate, with other records than those of P. C. Y. and contain indexes of administrations. The introductions to each volume should be consulted, for the records of P. C. Y., as well as all other probate records for the Province of York, are more complicated than might at first sight be apparent. For the period 1689-1730, no Calendars exist and one must therefore refer to the Probate and Administration Act Books to find a will or administration believed to have been ratified by P. C. Y. during this period. Inventories when found are usually with the filed will and are neither stored nor indexed separately.

Normally, the registered copy of a P. C. Y. will is produced to the searcher at the Borthwick Institute, St. Anthony's Hall, York, but, as with P. C. C., the original will be produced if there is no registered copy. If a searcher has good reason to see the original rather than the registered will, the original would generally be produced for inspection without fee, but up to about 1660 the original wills are in poor condition. Access to P. C. Y. records is not governed by quite such formality as is true of P. C. C., but is subject to such conditions as the Borthwick Institute may from time to time impose. Photographic copies of documents and transcripts are provided, under the same regulations and at the same cost as at the Principal Probate Registry.

Probate and Probate Records in Scotland

☼

SCOTLAND and England have widely differing legal systems. For the sake of completeness and because it is certain that wills of Virginian interest are to be found in Scottish probate records, some brief account of the position in Scotland must be given in this present report.

As in England, probate (known in Scotland as confirmation of testaments) and administration of intestates' estates began as an ecclesiastical responsibility and until 1560 was exercised by diocesan bishops, who delegated their jurisdiction in probate and other matters to ecclesiastical lawyers known as Officials or Commissaries, though it is understood that some rural deans in Scotland had probate jurisdiction. The Commissaries exercised their jurisdiction in districts known as Commissariots, which were usually coincident in area with the bishopric. The Diocese of St. Andrews was an exception, being split into two Commissariots.

The Commissary Court of Edinburgh held a place in Scotland similar to P. C. C. in England, in that wills of persons dying in England and overseas who left estate, real or personal, in Scotland were proved in that court as far as the Scottish estates were concerned. The records of this court may be expected to contain material of Virginian interest.

In 1876, confirmation of testaments, administration of intestates' estates and such remnants of their jurisdiction as still remained to Commissariot Courts were removed from them and the courts (except for that of Edinburgh) were abolished, their functions being transferred to the Sheriffs' Courts.

By an Act of Parliament of 1823 all testamentary records in the Commissariot Courts down to 1823 were ordered to be placed in the General Register House in Edinburgh, where they now are. Manuscript indexes from the earliest date to the date of transmittal for each of the twenty-two Commissariots were prepared by and are available in the Register House. Printed indexes down to 1800 have been published by the Scottish Record Society for all Commissariots except Caithness, Orkney and Zetland, Peebles, and Ross; for these Commissariots, the printed indexes cover the periods 1661-1664, 1611-1684, 1681-1699, and 1802-1824, respectively. Indexes have been printed by the British Record Society in their *Index Library* for Edinburgh, 1514-1600, Inverness, 1630-1800, and Hamilton and Campsie, 1564-1800.

A full list of all Commissariot Court records appears in M. Livingstone, *A Guide to the Public Records of Scotland* (Edinburgh, 1905), pp. 109-129.

Probate and Probate Records in Ireland

¤

ANY discussion of Irish probate records earlier than 1858 and, indeed, earlier than 1922 must now be largely academic, since almost all these records were destroyed in the catastrophic bombardment and burning of the record repository of the Public Record Office of Ireland in 1922. The policy pursued by the Irish record authorities in centralizing the country's archives in Dublin had by 1922 resulted in an intense concentration of documents in the Public Record Office, so that the losses resulting from the fire were immense. It is unfortunate in the extreme that the probate records were among those almost totally destroyed in the fire. Certain printed indexes of Irish wills were published before 1922 and some manuscript indexes still exist in the Record Office in Dublin, but as the records to which these refer no longer exist, the indexes are of little value except as indications of what once existed.

The arrangements for the proving of wills in Ireland were modelled on the English pattern to a large extent. Wills relating to estates in one diocese were proved in the court of the bishop of that diocese; wills relating to estates in more than one diocese and wills of persons with estates in Ireland, dying overseas, were proved in the Prerogative Court of the Archbishop of Armagh, who exercised a jurisdiction like that of the Archbishop of Canterbury in England. Similarly, letters of administration were granted by either the diocesan court or the Prerogative Court. Peculiar jurisdictions existed, but not to anywhere near the same extent as in England.

As in England, so in Ireland ecclesiastical jurisdiction in testamentary matters was ended by an Act of Parliament in 1858, when a Principal Probate Registry was established in Dublin, along with district probate registries covering virtually the same areas as the former diocesan jurisdictions. Most of the earlier records of these registries had by 1922 been centralized in the Public Record Office of Ireland. Since probate registries had to transfer records more than twenty years old to the Public Record Office of Ireland, in general those up to 1902 were destroyed. However, although the original wills and other papers connected with testamentary business may have disappeared, the district registries retained their transcript copies of wills, which can still be inspected at the offices of the registries.

Unfortunately, all the records of the Principal Probate Registry in Dublin, including the registers of wills for 1858-1902, had been transferred to the Public Record Office in Dublin by 1922 and thus no records of the Principal Registry earlier than 1903 now exist.

Other copies of wills after 1708, together with deeds and other conveyances of land in Ireland, are to be found entered among the records of the Registry of Deeds in Dublin, since these records were not considered within the scope of the Acts govering the Public Records of Ireland, and were not therefore in the Record Office in 1922 and remain still in the custody of the Registry. As far as is known no printed index to these records is generally available, but no doubt application to the Registry for information about the existence of a will would disclose whether it was in fact enrolled and whether a copy could be supplied.

With the partition of Ireland in 1922 into the Republic of Eire and the six northern counties, which form part of the United Kingdom, a second Irish record office, the Public Record Office of Northern Ireland, was established as the repository for records of the Government of Northern Ireland and of other public and private records in the six counties. Probate records later than 1922 for probate registries in Northern Ireland are the responsibility of the Public Record Office of Northern Ireland. Both Irish record offices, since 1922, have made a special point of attracting into their keeping original wills, probate copies of wills, and any other existing copies of wills relating to the areas for which they are responsible. It is therefore always possible that a copy of a will, whose existence has been disclosed by manuscript or printed index, may now be in one or the other of these record offices, and enquiry should be made of both.

Information on what probate records were in the Public Record Office in Dublin immediately before the 1922 disaster will be found in Herbert Wood, *A Guide to the Records Deposited in the Public Record Office of Ireland* (Dublin, 1919). For a note of what survived the fire, *The Fifty-Fifth Report of the Deputy Keeper of the Public Records and Keeper of the State Papers in Ireland* (Dublin, 1928) should be consulted. An early indication of the way in which the *lacunae* after 1922 were being supplied is contained in The Reverend Wallace Clare, ed., *Irish Genealogical Guides. A Guide to Copies & Abstracts of Irish Wills,* First Series, Vol. I (March, Cambridgeshire, 1930). Enquiries in Dublin and Belfast may indicate other volumes of the series or of a similar kind.

Between 1895 and 1922 were published indexes to wills of a number of Irish dioceses down to 1800, and, for some dioceses, indexes all the way up to 1858. These indexes may have interest for the student, although the chances of survival of copies of wills in any form in Dublin or Belfast are not very great.

Appendix to the Second Edition

The Present Whereabouts of English and Welsh Probate Records Earlier Than 1858

Address changes and other revisions in the following list were made based on information printed in much greater detail in J. S. W. Gibson, comp., *Wills and Where to Find Them* (Chichester, Eng., 1974).

Name of Court	*Present place of deposit of its records*
Episcopal Consistory of St. Asaph Episcopal Consistory of Bangor Peculiar of Hawarden	National Library of Wales, Aberystwyth
Episcopal Consistory of Lichfield Dean and Chapter of Lichfield Peculiar of Dean of Lichfield Lichfield Peculiars	Joint Record Office, Public Library, Bird Street, Lichfield WS13 6PN
Knowle Manor	Warwickshire Record Office, Shire Hall, Warwick
Archdeaconry of Northampton Episcopal Consistory of Peterborough, Western Division	Northamptonshire Record Office, Delapre Abbey, Northampton NN4 9AW
Archdeaconry of Bedford Peculiar of Biggleswade Peculiar of Leighton Buzzard	County Record Office, County Hall, Bedford MK42 9AP
Episcopal Consistory of Worcester Dean and Chapter of Worcester Worcester Peculiars	Worcestershire Record Office, St. Helen's Church, Fish Street, Worcester

Episcopal Consistory of Bristol, Dorset Division Archdeaconry of Dorset Dorset Peculiars (all)	Dorset Record Office, County Hall, Dorchester, DT1 1XJ
Consistorial Court of Archdeaconry of Cornwall Royal Peculiar of St. Buryan	Cornwall County Record Office, County Hall, Truro TR1 3AY
Consistory of Bishop of Bristol in Deanery of Bristol	Bristol Archives Office, The Council House, Bristol BS1 5TR
Episcopal Consistory of Canterbury Archdeaconry of Canterbury	Kent Archives Office, County Hall, Maidstone, Kent ME14 1XH
Episcopal Consistory of Carlisle Manor of Temple Sowerby Manor of Ravenstonedale	Archives Department, Cumbria County Council, The Record Office, The Castle, Carlisle
Episcopal Consistory of St. Davids	National Library of Wales, Aberystwyth
Episcopal Consistory of Chester	(a) Wills relating to Cheshire: Cheshire Record Office, The Castle, Chester CH1 2DN (b) Wills relating to Lancaster and Yorkshire: Lancaster Record Office, Sessions House, Lancaster Road, Preston PR1 2RE
Palatine Episcopal Consistory of Durham Peculiars of Bishop of Durham and of the Dean in Allerton and Allertonshire Peculiar of Crayke	The Department of Palaeography and Diplomatic, University of Durham, South Road, Durham DH1 3LE

Episcopal Principal Registry of Exeter Episcopal Consistory of Exeter Consistory of Archdeacon of Exeter Consistory of Archdeacon of Barnstaple Consistory of Archdeacon of Totnes Consistory of Dean and Chapter of Exeter Peculiar of Dean of Exeter Peculiar of Custos of Cathedral and Vicars Choral	All records destroyed by enemy action during World War II
Episcopal Consistory of Bath and Wells Consistory of Archdeacon of Wells Consistory of Archdeacon of Taunton Consistory of Dean and Chapter of Wells Consistory of Dean of Wells All Wells Peculiars and Prebends	Somerset Record Office, Obridge Road, Taunton TA2 7PU
Episcopal Consistory of Gloucester Peculiar of Rector of Bibury Peculiar of Rector of Bishops Cleeve	Gloucestershire Record Office, Archives Department, City Library, Brunswick Road, Gloucester GL1 1HT
Archdeaconry of Suffolk	Suffolk Record Office, County Hall, Ipswich IP4 2JS
Archdeaconry of Sudbury Peculiar of Isleham and Freckenham	Suffolk Record Office, School Hall Street, Bury St. Edmunds, IP33 1RX

Peculiar of the Liberty of the Sokens	Essex Record Office, County Hall, Chelmsford, Essex CM1 1LX
Commissary of the Archdeaconry of Richmond, Western Deaneries Manor of Halton	Lancashire Record Office, Sessions House, Lancaster Road, Preston PR1 2RE
Commissary of Bishop of Lincoln in Archdeaconry of Leicester and Court of the Archdeacon Prebend of St. Margaret in Leicester Commissaries of Rothley, Groby and Evington Prebends of Liddington, Caldecott and Ketton	Leicestershire Record Office 57 New Walk, Leicester LE1 7JB
Consistory of Bishop of Chichester in the Archdeanry of Lewes Deanery of Battle	East Sussex Record Office, Pelham House, Lewes, Sussex
Peculiar of the Archbishop of Canterbury in the Deanery of South Malling	West Sussex Record Office, John Edes House, West Street, Chichester PO19 1RN *and* East Sussex Record Office, Pelham House, Lewes, Sussex
Episcopal Consistory of Lincoln and Archdeacon of Lincoln Archdeaconry of Stow Dean and Chapter of Lincoln Peculiar of Subdean Prebends of Lincoln Manor of Kirkstead	Lincolnshire Archives Office, The Castle, Lincoln LN1 3AB

Episcopal Consistory of Llandaff Consistory of Archdeaconry of Brecon Episcopal Consistory of Hereford Consistory of Dean of Hereford Peculiar of Chancellor of Choir of Cathedral Peculiar Prebend of Moreton Magna Peculiar Prebend of Upper Bullinghope	National Library of Wales, Aberystwyth
Prerogative Court of Canterbury	Public Record Office, Chancery Lane, London WC2A 1LR
Archdeaconry of St. Albans	Hertfordshire Record Office, County Hall, Hertford SG13 8DE
Court of Arches, Canterbury	Lambeth Palace Library, London SE1 7JU
Peculiar of the Archbishop of Canterbury in the Deaneries of the Arches, Shoreham and Croydon	Lambeth Palace Library, London SE1 7JU
Archdeaconry of Berkshire	Department of Western MSS, Bodleian Library, Oxford OX1 3BG
Archdeaconry of Buckinghamshire	Buckinghamshire Record Office, County Offices, Aylesbury HP20 1UA
Peculiar of Rector of Cliffe	Kent Archives Office, County Hall, Maidstone, Kent ME14 1XH

Archdeaconry of Colchester Archdeaconry of Essex Essex Peculiars (Bocking, Writtle, Good Easter)	Essex Record Office, County Hall, Chelmsford, Essex CM1 1LX
Archdeaconry of Huntingdon, Herts Division	Huntingdonshire Record Office, County Buildings, Huntingdon
Court of Hustings	Corporation of London Record Office, Guildhall, London EC2P 2EJ
Royal Peculiar of St. Katherine by the Tower Commissary of London, London Division	Guildhall Library, Basinghall Street, London EC2P 2EJ
Commissary of London, Essex and Herts Divisions	Essex Record Office, County Hall, Chelmsford, Essex CM1 1LX
Archdeaconry of London	Guildhall Library, Basinghall Street, London EC2P 2EJ
Episcopal Consistory of London Archdeaconry of Middlesex	Greater London Record Office, Room B21, County Hall, Westminster Bridge, London SE1 7PB
Episcopal Consistory and Archdeaconry of Oxford Oxon and Bucks (and some Berks) Peculiars	Department of Western MSS, Bodleian Library, Oxford OX1 3BG
Peculiars of the Dean and Chapter at St. Paul's	The Library, St. Paul's Cathedral, London EC4
Episcopal Consistory of Rochester and Archdeaconry of Rochester	Kent Archives Office, County Hall, Maidstone, Kent ME14 1XH

Episcopal Consistory of Sarum Archdeaconry of Sarum Peculiar of Dean of Sarum Sarum Peculiars (all)	Wiltshire Record Office, County Hall, Trowbridge, Wiltshire BA14 8JG
Commissary of Bishop of Winchester in Archdeaconry of Surrey Archdeaconry of Surrey	Greater London Record Office, Room B21, County Hall, Westminster Bridge, London SE1 7PB
Royal Peculiar of Dean and Chapter of Westminster	City of Westminster Archives Department, Public Library, Buckingham Palace Road, London SW1
Archdeaconry of Wiltshire	Wiltshire Record Office, County Hall, Trowbridge, Wiltshire BA14 8JG
Episcopal Consistory of Norwich Archdeaconry of Norwich Archdeaconry of Norfolk Peculiar of Dean and Chapter of Norwich	Norfolk Record Office, Central Library, Bethel Street, Norwich NOR 57E
Peculiar of the Collegiate Church of Southwell Manor of Mansfield Manor of Bawtry Peculiar of Kinoulton Manor of Dale Abbey	Nottinghamshire Record Office, County House, High Pavement, Nottingham NG1 1HR
Commissary of Bishop of Lincoln in Archdeaconry of Huntingdon and Archdeacon's Court Huntingdon Peculiars	Huntingdonshire Record Office, County Buildings, Huntingdon

Episcopal Consistory of Ely	Archivist to the Bishop and Dean and Chapter of Ely, Cambridge University Library, West Road, Cambridge CB3 9DR
Archdeaconry of Ely Court of Chancellor of University of Cambridge Manor of Thorney	Keeper of the University Archives, Cambridge University Library, West Road, Cambridge CB3 9DR
Rutland Peculiar—Empringham Northants Peculiar—Nassington	Lincolnshire Archives Office, The Castle, Lincoln LN1 3AB
Salop Peculiars (except Prees or Pipe Manor)	National Library of Wales, Aberystwyth
Prees or Pipe Manor	Lichfield Joint Record Office, Public Library, Bird Street, Lichfield WS13 6PN
Episcopal Consistory and Archdeaconry Courts of Winchester Hants Peculiars	Hampshire Record Office, 20 Southgate St., (St. Thomas Church), Winchester S023 9EF
Episcopal Consistory for Archdeaconry of Chichester Peculiar of Dean of Chichester Peculiar Deaneries of Pagham and Tarring	West Sussex Record Office, John Edes House, West Street, Chichester P019 IRN
Prerogative Court of Archbishop of York and Exchequer Court of the Dean Episcopal Consistory and Chancery Courts of York Court of Dean and Chapter of York Peculiar of Dean of York	Borthwick Institute, St. Anthony's Hall, Peaseholme Green, York Y01 2PW

Peculiars of Chancellor,
Precentor, Subdean and
succentor of Cathedral
Peculiar of Archdeacon of York
Peculiar of Archdeacon of East
Riding
Further York Peculiars (except
Kinoulton and Southwell—for
which see earlier in list)

Peculiar of Archbishop of York in Hexham, Hexhamshire and Ripon	Borthwick Institute, St. Anthony's Hall, Peaseholme Green, York Y01 2PW *and* Northumberland Record Office, Melton Park, North Gosforth, Newcastle-upon-Tyne NE3 5QX
Commissary of Archdeacon of Richmond, Eastern Deaneries	Leeds Archives Department, Sheepscar Library, Leeds LS7 3AP